The Butterfl

Classroom Questions

A SCENE BY SCENE TEACHING GUIDE

Amy Farrell

SCENE BY SCENE

ENNISKERRY, IRELAND

Scene by Scene
Wicklow, Ireland.
www.scenebysceneguides.com

The Butterfly Lion Classroom Questions by Amy Farrell.
ISBN 978-1-910949-72-6

Contents

Chapter One
'Chilblains and Semolina Pudding'

Summary

The speaker begins by telling us that to see butterflies, you must be in the right place at the right time, as was the case when he saw the butterfly lion.

He is ten years old, away at boarding school, and he hates it.

He dreads Basher Beaumont, who bullies him.

He is homesick after receiving a letter from his mother. He is also feeling miserable because Basher Beaumont smeared his hair in shoe polish and Mr Carter put him standing in a corner with a book on his head for the whole lesson. He decides to run away.

He leaves the following Sunday afternoon, climbing the fence and running for it. He plans to walk to the train station and go home to London.

He sees a huge, ivy covered wall and a stone archway with a great stone lion.

Hearing a car, he pushes open the iron gate and slips through.

He does not want to be caught and caned, or sent back to school to face detentions and Basher Beaumont.

Deeming the road to be too dangerous, he decides to cut across country to reach the train station.

Questions

1. What does the speaker tell us about butterflies as the chapter begins?

2. How did the speaker come to see the butterfly lion?

3. How does he describe the butterfly lion?

4. What age was the speaker when he saw the butterfly lion?

5. Does the speaker like boarding school? Why/why not?
   Does it sound appealing to you?
   Give reasons for your answer.

6. Who is Basher Beaumont?

7. Why is the narrator, "more miserable than I had ever been before"?
   Would you feel the same way, in his position?

8. What does the speaker decide to do about his situation?
   Does this sound like a good idea to you?

9. How does the narrator get off the school grounds?

10. Where does he plan to go next?

11. Describe the "high brick wall" beyond the grass verge.
    What, do you think, lies behind it?

12. Describe the gateway at the bend of the road.

13.   Why does the speaker push open the gate?

14.   What will happen if he is caught running away?

15.   How will he get to the train station?
Is this a better idea than going along the road, do you think?

16.   What are your first impressions of the narrator, based on this opening chapter?
Include examples in your answer.

17.   If you were the illustrator of this story, what illustrations would you include for this chapter?

18.   How does the opening chapter arouse your curiosity and make you want to read more?
What questions do you have, so far?

Chapter Two
'Strange Meeting'

Summary

The narrator hears a voice behind him. It is an old lady and her growling dog. She tells him he is on private property. Seeing his uniform, she realises he has run away from school.

She invites him in for tea. Her house is huge and covered in ivy. They sit by the stove in the kitchen where she prepares tea and scones.

He eats three scones while the old lady talks to him. Through the window, he notices a rainbow and a lion shaped shadow.

She tells him that the clouds always go away in the end, before suggesting that she return him to his school.

The lion on the hillside is still there, but now it is blue and shimmering. The old lady says he is real, that he belongs to her and Bertie.

She offers to take the narrator to Africa, by telling him her story.

The narrator is no longer hungry, wanting to hear her story. She tells it slowly, looking at the butterfly lion as she does so.

Questions

1. Describe the old lady the speaker meets.

2. How is her dog behaving?

3. How does she react to his school uniform?

4. Why does the narrator go with the old lady?
   What would you do here, in his position?

5. Describe the old lady's house.

6. What does she offer the narrator?

7. What are your first impressions of this old lady?

8. Does the narrator enjoy the tea and scones?

9. What does he see out of the window behind the old lady?

10. What does the old lady say about the sun coming out?
    Is this good advice, do you think?

11. Why does the old lady say that he must go back to school?
    How would you feel, if you were the boy?

12. Who is Bertie?

13. Describe the lion the narrator sees on the hillside.

14. What does the old lady offer to tell the boy about?
    Is he interested in her story?

15.   How does she tell her story?

16.   What details in this chapter make you curious to read more?

Chapter Three
'Timbavati'

Summary

Bertie was born in South Africa, where his father was a farmer.

When Bertie started walking, they put a fence around the farmhouse to keep him safe from leopards, lions and spotted hyenas.

The farm was twenty thousand acres, but times were hard because of drought and lion and leopard attacks on the cattle.

His father often had to go to guard the cattle. He always told Bertie not to open the gate as he left, because of the wild animals.

Bertie's mother also warned him to stay inside the gate. As there was no school nearby, his mother was also his teacher.

She was often sick with malaria, but she had good days too. On her rare good days, she played with him, or talked about her home in England and the loneliness of Africa.

When she was not well and happy, Bertie was left to his own devices.

He spent hours watching the animals visiting a waterhole downhill from the farmhouse.

He longed for the arrival of a pride of lions to the waterhole.

He begged his mother to take him out of the compound, but she never did, as his father had forbidden it.

The men used to come home with stories of cheetahs, leopards, hyenas and elephants.

Bertie asked his father to take him with him, but his father laughed, saying it was man's work.

Bertie decided to go into the veld himself, but something always held him back. The stories of dangerous animals kept him inside the fence.

One evening when he was six, he saw a white lion cub follow a lioness to the waterhole. His parents did not believe him when he told them about it, saying there is no such thing as a white lion.

Bertie watched for the white lion cub over the next few days, but did not see it.

Bertie's father rode into the compound, delighted to have got a huge lioness that had been taking his cattle. Bertie knew instantly that his white lion cub had been orphaned.

Bertie promised himself that if the lion cub came to the waterhole, he would take it home.

He waited for the cub each day, but he did not come.

Questions

1.   Where was Bertie born?
     Do you know anything about this part of the world?

2.   Why did Bertie's parents decide to fence in their
     farmhouse?

3.   Describe Bertie's farm.

4.   What made farming difficult?

5.   Why did Bertie's father have to spend time away from
     home?

6.   What did Bertie's father say to him every time he left?
     What does this tell you about where they lived?

7.   Why was Bertie's mother also his teacher?
     Would you like to be taught by your mother instead of
     going to school?
     Give reasons for your answer.

8.   How was Bertie's mother's health?

9.   What were good days like with Bertie's mother?

10. Did Bertie's mother like Africa?
     Do you understand why she felt this way?

11. Why was Bertie often left to his own devices?
     How does this make you feel?

12.   Why was the waterhole Bertie's whole world?

13.   What did Bertie always long for when watching the waterhole?

14.   Why was Bertie never lonely as a child?
Would you be lonely, if you were him?

15.   Why wouldn't Bertie's mother take him outside the compound?

16.   What stories did the men tell of the veld?
Do these stories sound interesting to you?

17.   How did Bertie's father respond when Bertie asked to go with him guarding cattle?
How would this make you feel, if you were Bertie?

18.   What did Bertie's father teach him to do?

19.   What stopped Bertie from going into the veld by himself?

20.   Why did Bertie's compound feel like a prison to him?

21.   What interesting sight did he see at the waterhole one evening when he was six?

22.   How did Bertie's father respond when Bertie told him what he saw?
How does this make you feel?

23. How did Bertie's mother respond to what he saw?
How does this make you feel?

24. What animal did Bertie's father shoot?
Why did he do this?
Why was Bertie's mother concerned about this?

25. How did Bertie feel about what happened?
Was he angry with his father? Why/why not?
Would you be? Why/why not?

26. What did Bertie hear that night?

27. What did Bertie promise himself?

28. The lion cub did not come to the waterhole.
What could this mean?

29. What makes this an exciting chapter?

30. Would you like to have had a childhood like Bertie's?
Give reasons for your answer.

Chapter Four
'Bertie and the Lion'

Summary

Bertie was woken by zebras neighing as hyenas scattered them from the waterhole. He saw three hyenas moving in on a muddy lion cub.

Bertie ran to the waterhole, yelling and screaming. The hyenas backed off at first, but then began to circle Bertie.

Bertie's mother fired her rifle to scare the hyenas off. She ran to him in her nightgown and together they brought the cub home. They fed and cleaned him.

When Bertie's father came home, both Bertie and his mother asked to keep the cub. She spoke with a strength and determination Bertie had not heard before.

That night, Bertie listened to his parents argue about the lion cub. His mother said the lion would be a playmate for Bertie, who would never have siblings. His father gave in and agreed to keep the cub.

The lion cub lived in the farmhouse, sleeping on Bertie's bed and following him everywhere.

Bertie was totally happy, the lion cub was all he needed.

Bertie's mother was very patient with the lion. She was rarely ill these days.

Bertie's father said the lion should live outside the compound, but he stayed where he was, bringing life and laughter to Bertie and his mother.

Questions

1. What woke Bertie a week or so later?
   What was going on?
   What would you do, if you were Bertie?

2. Describe the lion cub.

3. What were the hyenas about to do?

4. How did Bertie react?

5. What made the hyenas run away?

6. Was Bertie brave or foolish to have run to the lion cub
   like this?
   Would you do this, in his position?

7. Who fired the shot that scared the hyenas?
   What is your response to this?

8. How did Bertie and his mother care for the lion cub?

9. Bertie and his mother wanted to keep the cub.
   What is your response to this?

10. What did Bertie notice about his mother's voice here?
    What is your response to this?

11. How did Bertie's father feel about keeping the lion?

12. What did Bertie do when he was supposed to be in bed?

13. What objections did Bertie's father have to keeping the cub?

14. What arguments did Bertie's mother make in favour of the cub?

15. What do you learn about Bertie's family from his parents' conversation here?

16. Where did the lion cub sleep?

17. What did Bertie feed the cub?

18. Why was Bertie totally happy?

19. Why didn't Bertie give the lion a name?

20. How did Bertie's mother treat the lion cub?

21. What change did Bertie notice in his mother? Can you explain this change?

22. How did Bertie's father feel about the lion?

23. What is the mood like as the chapter ends?

24. Would you like to have a pet lion? Why/why not?

25. What is the most unusual pet that you have come across?

Were they a good pet? Explain what makes you say this.

Chapter Five
'Running Free'

Summary

A year later, Bertie is to be sent to England to attend school.

He knew something was up as his mother seemed sad recently.

His father broke the news after returning from Johannesburg. Bertie was to be sent to school in Salisbury, and would live with his aunt and uncle during school holidays.

His mother would sail to England with him in July and return to the farm in September.

Bertie's heart filled with dread. He asked what was to become of the lion.

His father arranged for a French circus owner to come and take a look at the lion.

Bertie shouted at his father, enraged.

His mother said they always knew they could not keep him forever, and added that he could not fend for himself in the veld.

Bertie said he promised the lion that he would never be behind bars. He did not want people to laugh at the lion.

He knew that his parents' minds were made up.

That night, he took his father's rifle and the lion, and left the compound. He saw a herd of elephants and ran for it, running until he could go no further.

At daybreak he told the lion to be wild, and not to come home ever again.

However, the lion followed Bertie, even when he threw sticks and stones, and shouted at it.

With no other option, Bertie fired the rifle and the lion scampered away.

Bertie did not care how he would be punished, he was glad to have given the lion a chance at freedom.

Questions

1.   How did Bertie know there was "something in the wind"?

2.   What was his father's lecture about?

3.   What plans had been made for Bertie's schooling? Do these plans surprise you?

4.   How did Bertie feel about these plans? How would you feel, in his position?

5.   What would happen to Bertie's lion? How do you feel about this?

6.   How did Bertie react when he heard his father's plans for his lion?

7.   Why didn't they release the lion into the veld?

8.   Why was Bertie so against the idea of a circus? Do you agree or disagree with Bertie's point of view? Give reasons for your answer.

9.   Were Bertie's parents doing the right thing for their son here, in your opinion? What alternatives were available to them?

10.   What did Bertie do that night? Was this a good idea, in your opinion?

11. Why did Bertie run when he saw a herd of elephants wandering towards them?

12. What did Bertie do as the sun came up?
How was he feeling?
Do you feel sorry for him here?
Give reasons for your answer.

13. Why did Bertie throw stones and sticks at the lion?
How must Bertie be feeling?
How must the lion be feeling?

14. Why, do you think, did Bertie shout "I hate you!" at the lion?
How does this make you feel?

15. What made Bertie fire the rifle?

16. How did the lion respond to the gunfire?

17. Would Bertie be punished for freeing the lion like this?

18. What is the mood like as this chapter ends?
Explain your answer fully.

19. In this chapter, Bertie learned that he was to be sent to another country to live and attend school.
What are your views on this arrangement?
How would you feel about this if you were Bertie's parents?

Chapter Six
'The Frenchman'

Summary

Bertie's parents were waiting when he got home. He was sent to his room.

His father looked for the lion each day, and was furious when he could not find him.

Bertie spent his days watching for the lion. He prayed that the lion would fend for himself and not return until after the Frenchman's visit.

The lion returned in a pitiful state, just as the Frenchman was being told it had escaped.

The lion was soaked to the skin, trembling and very thin.

The Frenchman was thrilled with the lion, saying he would be the star of his show. He promised to care for the lion, but this did not make Bertie feel any better.

Bertie realised that the lion would have to go with the Frenchman, as it could not survive in the wild.

That night, he promised the lion that he would find him.

The Frenchman invited Bertie to visit his circus in France, before leaving with the lion in a crate.

When he left for school a few months later, Bertie was not unhappy, as England is closer to France than Africa is.

Questions

1. What happened when Bertie arrived home?
   Were you surprised that he did not get into more trouble?

2. What mood was Bertie's father in when he returned from his searches for the lion?

3. Bertie's father said he should "strap" him.
   What does this mean?
   What stopped Bertie's father from following through on this threat, in your opinion?

4. How did Bertie spend his time?

5. What did Bertie pray for?

6. What happened when the Frenchman arrived?
   Why was the timing here unlucky?

7. What condition was the lion in?

8. How does the weather add to this scene?

9. What did the Frenchman think of the lion?

10. Describe the Frenchman's face.

11. Why didn't the Frenchman's promise to care for the lion make Bertie feel any better?

12. Why did Bertie decide that the lion would have to go with the Frenchman?

13. What promise did Bertie make the lion?
How does this make you feel?

14. What invitation did the Frenchman extend before leaving?

15. How will the lion be transported?

16. How did Bertie feel about leaving Africa?
What made him feel this way?

17. What makes this a sad chapter?
Include examples in your answer.

Chapter Seven
'Strawbridge'

Summary

The old lady wrinkles her nose at her cold tea. From this point, she says, the story is not just Bertie's, but hers too.

The boy asks about the white lion. The old lady is sad and asks if he wants the truth or a happy story. He chooses the truth.

The old lady grew up in the grand house at Strawbridge. She was mostly alone as a child. Her mother died in childbirth and her father was seldom home.

From the moment they met, she and Bertie got on well together.

She had few friends and did not attend school, being taught by a governess. Nanny Mason brought her up.

She had lessons with Nolips each morning and walked with Nanny Mason in the afternoon. She was allowed to spend Sunday alone if her father was not home.

She spent this time flying kites and reading books.

She was trying to fly a kite on the day she met Bertie. Her kite got tangled in an elm tree and Bertie retrieved it for her.

He offered to fix it for her. She realised he was from the nearby school. He asked her not to tell on him, saying he had run away and was not going back.

He told her about Africa and his lion being sent to the circus.

She was unsure whether she believed him.

He said he would not be able to take the lion home when he found him as his mother had died and his father had re-married. Bertie did not want to go home ever again.

She told him he should go back to school before he was missed. He agreed to, if he could come and visit her again.

They began to meet every Sunday.

Bertie was not worried about getting caught, he said one more beating would not make much difference and he would be happy to be expelled.

Questions

1. What makes the old lady wrinkle her nose in disgust?

2. What is different about the old lady's story from this point?
    What does this mean, do you think?

3. What does the narrator want to know about?
    Would you feel the same way, if you were him?

4. What does the old lady say about true stories?

5. What choice of story does she offer the boy?
    Which would you choose?
    Give a reason for your answer.

6. What was the old lady's childhood like?

7. What did she have in common with Bertie?

8. Who were Miss Tulips and Nanny Mason?

9. How did she spend her days, as a child?

10. How did she spend her free time?

11. Does it sound like the old lady had a fun childhood to you?

12. Why did she enjoy reading so much?

13. What was she doing on the day she met Bertie?

14. What difficulty did she run into?
How did she respond to this difficulty?

15. What did Bertie do for her?

16. How did Bertie react when she noticed his school uniform?

17. What was Bertie doing out of school?
Who does he remind you of here?

18. Where was Bertie planning to go?
How does this make you feel?

19. How did they spend that first afternoon together?

20. What has happened to Bertie's mother?
Why did this happen, according to Bertie?

21. What has Bertie's father done?

22. "I never want to go back."
Would you want to go home, if you were Bertie?
Explain your reasons fully.

23. How would you feel, in Bertie's position?

24. What made Bertie go back to school?

25. How did the children arrange to see each other?

26. Why did Bertie come through the woods?

27.   Was Bertie worried about getting caught?

28.   What was life like for Bertie at boarding school?
        What is your response to this?

29.   Are you glad that the children became friends?
        Give a reason for your answer.

Chapter Eight
'And All's Well'

Summary

They met every Sunday after that. Sometimes they did not have much time together because Bertie had detention or her father was shooting pheasants with friends.

Over the next two years they became best friends. The girl believed everything Bertie told her about Africa and the lion.

School holidays dragged without Bertie.

Millie's nature walks with Nanny Mason were boring compared to how she pictured Africa.

The children did not write to each other, for fear of their letters being found and read.

As time went on, Bertie spoke less about the white lion.

They had one last term together, before they were to be sent away to different schools. They treasured their time together.

Bertie gave Millie a kite on their last Sunday together and said she was to think of him when she flew it.

They went to their different schools. Millie was careful with the kite, for fear of losing it.

Bertie and Millie wrote to each other.

He was unhappy at college.

They both dreaded the threat of war.

Millie's father went off to war and they never saw him again. Millie was sad, but did not grieve much for her father, as she never really knew him.

Millie hoped that the war would end before Bertie was old enough to be sent to war.

In his last letter to her from college, he told her that he was signing up. He wanted to be free and this was the only way for him to be so.

He told her he would think of her always, whatever happened.

Questions

1. Why were the children sometimes short of time when they met on Sundays?

2. How did they spend their time together?

3. Did the children get on well together?

4. What did Bertie tell the girl (Millie) "again and again"? What does this suggest to you?

5. What made the school holidays drag?

6. Did the girl enjoy her nature walks with Nanny Mason?

7. How did Nanny Mason react to Millie's (the girl's) knowledge of Africa?

8. What stopped Bertie and Millie from writing to each other?

9. What did Bertie and Millie talk about all the time?

10. What did Bertie begin to talk about less? Why was this the case, do you think?

11. Where were they being sent after one last summer together? Why was this the case?

12.	"We treasured each meeting..."
	Describe Millie and Bertie's relationship at this point.

13.	What gift did Bertie give to Millie on their last Sunday
	together?

14.	Why was Millie careful when she flew Bertie's kite?
	Can you explain what made her feel this way?

15.	Why did Bertie and Millie write to each other now?

16.	What were Millie's letters like?

17.	What were Bertie's letters like?

18.	Have you ever sent someone a letter?
	In what way is a letter better than a phonecall?

19.	Why were their letters full of dread?

20.	Why did Millie never see her father again?
	What happened to him?

21.	Was Millie very upset?
	Does her reaction here surprise you?

22.	What was Millie more concerned about?

23.	What did Bertie's last letter from college tell Millie?

24.	What were Bertie's reasons for signing up?
	What is your response to this?

25.   Bertie told Millie that she remembered a boy, as they
        had not seen each other in so long.
        How does this make you feel?

Chapter Nine
'A Lot of Old Codswallop'

Summary

While the boy lets out the dog, the old lady goes and gets the kite Bertie made her.

It is huge and dusty, made of brown canvas. The old lady says it still flies.

The boy wants to hear about the white lion. She tells him to look outside. When he looks he sees that the lion on the hillside is white now, not blue.

The boy wants to know about the lion in the story. The old lady says it is the same lion, before continuing with her story.

For years, Bertie could not speak of his wartime experience.

He had marched into France full of hope and expectation, but found himself huddled under heavy fire, and marching into No Man's Land to be shot at any moment.

On Bertie's twentieth birthday, he and his men counter-attacked fleeing German soldiers.

Bertie was hit in the leg and fell into a shellhole. His wound was bleeding badly, so he decided to crawl back to the trenches.

Despite his own wounds, he rescued two of his men, returning to No Man's Land for the second soldier. He was cheered on by both sides, German and British alike.

He woke up in hospital, with the men saved. He was awarded the Victoria Cross for his bravery under fire.

He called this award a lot of old codswallop, saying he did not have time to think when he saved them, so it was not really being brave.

His leg did not heal as well as it should. Bertie was still in hospital when Millie found him.

She found it very difficult, not hearing from Bertie for so long. She dreaded seeing Bertie's face among those of the wounded men returning from France.

Millie checked the newspaper lists of the killed and missing for Bertie's name. She was thankful never to find it, but worried because he had not written.

She decided to become a nurse and go to France, hoping to find Bertie.

Millie discovered how hopeless finding him would be amongst so many men in uniform, when she did not know his rank or regiment.

Her hospital was near Amiens. It was a converted chateau and was very cold in winter. They were short of doctors and medicine, but did all they could for the terribly wounded men.

She saw an article about Bertie in a magazine one morning. Millie cycled to the hospital where he was recovering and found him.

Questions

1. Where does the old lady go?

2. Describe the kite Bertie made for her.

3. Why is the boy disappointed by the kite?

4. What does the boy want to know about?
   Would you be impatient too, if you were him?

5. What is different about the lion on the hillside when the boy looks outside?

6. What is the dog chasing?

7. What does the old lady say about the lion on the hillside and the one in the story?
   Does the boy understand what she means?
   Do you know what is going on here?

8. What stopped Bertie from speaking about the fighting in the trenches for many years?

9. What was it like, marching out to war?
   How did things change for Bertie?

10. What did the soldiers do when the whistle blew?

11. What was 'No Man's Land'?

12.   What happened on the morning of Bertie's twentieth birthday?

13.   How was Bertie injured?

14.   Why did he decide to crawl back to the trenches?

15.   What stopped him from crawling to safety?

16.   Why did the stretcher-bearers try to take Bertie away? What did Bertie do instead?

17.   Why did the firing stop when Bertie went out into No Man's Land?

18.   Both sides, British and German, cheered Bertie on. What is your response to this? What does this suggest about people?

19.   Where did Bertie find himself when he woke up?

20.   What honour was Bertie awarded?

21.   How did Bertie respond to this award? What made him respond this way?

22.   What did Bertie compare saving the men to?

23.   What problem did Bertie have with his leg?

24.   Describe Bertie's wartime experience. Does it sound exciting or terrifying to you? Give reasons for your answer.

25.   "It was not entirely by accident that I found him."
        How does this line make you feel?

26.   What was it like for Millie, not hearing from Bertie?

27.   Was Nanny Mason a good friend to Millie at this time?

28.   Why was Millie miserable?

29.   What made Millie decide to become a nurse?
        What does this tell you about Millie?

30.   Why was it hopeless for Millie to go looking for Bertie
        in France?

31.   Where was Millie sent to?
        Was it a good hospital?

32.   What made it difficult to care for the wounded
        soldiers?

33.   What did Millie discover in the *Illustrated London News*?

34.   How did Millie and Bertie greet one another?
        What is your response to this?

Chapter Eleven
'The White Prince'

Summary

On Sundays Millie took Bertie to a nearby village. She pushed his wheelchair, they sat and talked or walked and talked.

Bertie explained that he did not write to Millie in the hope that she would forget about him and would not have to grieve for him.

One Sunday they saw a circus poster advertising The White Prince. They asked a cafe owner about the poster. He told them that the owner had to close the circus, but kept the animals. His home was bombarded and many animals were killed.

The army took the animals' food, so the owner shot them all, except The White Prince.

The cafe owner directed them to the circus owner's home, but he did not know if they were there anymore, or if they were even alive.

Millie and Bertie hitched a lift with an army truck to the circus owner's damaged house.

The house frightened Millie and she wanted to leave, but Bertie would not hear of it. He could smell the lion.

Monsieur Merlot lay propped up on a bed. The lion sprang from the bed and almost knocked Bertie over, rubbing up against him and yowling.

Questions

1. Why was it just like their old Sundays when they were little?

2. Describe the nearby village.

3. How did Bertie and Millie spend their time together?

4. What reason did Bertie give Millie for not writing to her?
   Is this a good reason, in your opinion?

5. What poster did they see one Sunday?
   How did Bertie react when he saw it?

6. What happened when Bertie tried to ask the cafe owner about the circus?

7. How did Millie help Bertie here?

8. Why did the circus close?

9. Why were many of the circus animals dead?
   How does this make you feel?

10. Why did the circus owner keep The White Prince?

11. "I think they die together. Maybe they die already. Who knows?"
    How do you feel at this point in the story?

12.   How did Bertie and Millie get to the circus owner's
        house?

13.   What condition was the house in when they got there?

14.   What makes this a tense moment in the story?

15.   What did Millie think of the house?

16.   How did Bertie know that the lion was there?

17.   How did the lion react to seeing Bertie?
        How does this make you feel?

Chapter Twelve
'A Miracle, A Miracle'

Summary

The lion grunted and groaned with pleasure as Bertie scratched him.

Monsieur Merlot was surprised to see Bertie before him.

He said he did all he could, but the lion is just skin and bones.

Bertie promised to feed them both and took Monsieur Merlot and the lion with him.

An ambulance gave them a lift back to the village, where Bertie bought a bone for the lion and a meal for Monsieur Merlot.

A crowd gathered to watch them. Millie was amazed, but not surprised by the morning's events. Bertie said he would find the lion, and now he had.

He brought the lion and Monsieur Merlot back to the hospital and asked a colonel if they could stay there until Bertie brought the lion to England.

At first the colonel was annoyed, until he recognised Bertie. Bertie said that if the lion was not looked after, it would have to be shot, and that shooting the symbol of Britain would be bad for morale.

It was difficult to persuade the powers that be to allow the lion home, but somehow Bertie managed it.

Photographers and reporters greeted them in Dover.

Bertie and Millie married in the village church and lived in Strawbridge.

Nanny Mason adored Bertie and the lion.

Questions

1. How did the lion behave around Bertie?

2. How did Monsieur Merlot respond to seeing Bertie?

3. How did the lion react to Millie?

4. How did she feel about the lion?

5. How did Monsieur Merlot feel about what happened to his animals?

6. Why did Millie keep her distance from the lion?

7. What condition was the lion in?

8. How did they get back to the village?

9. What did Bertie feed the lion and Monsieur Merlot?

10. Are you surprised that a crowd gathered around them?

11. Why did Millie take everything that happened that morning in her stride?

12. Comment on the image of Bertie leaning on the lion, Millie pushing Monsieur Merlot in the wheelchair and the crowd parting for them.

13. What request did Bertie make of the colonel at the hospital?

14.   How did the colonel react at first?

15.   How did Bertie persuade the colonel to agree?
        Was Bertie clever here?

16.   How did Bertie persuade the powers that be to allow
        the lion home?

17.   What reception did they receive at Dover?
        Why were they such big news, do you think?

18.   What disagreement did Bertie have with the vicar on
        his wedding day?

19.   How did Nanny Mason feel about Bertie and the lion?

20.   Are you happy with how things turned out for Millie,
        Bertie and the lion?
        Fully explain your point of view.

Chapter Thirteen
'The Butterfly Lion'

Summary

The lion roamed the park and chased deer and rabbits at Strawbridge, but never learned to kill them.

He ate venison and slept on a sofa on the landing.

Bertie's leg never healed properly and when it was bad, he needed something to lean on. It caused him a lot of pain, particularly in cold, damp weather.

On Sundays they walked the park together and Millie flew kites.

The lion never tried to escape, wanting always to be with Bertie.

The lion lived to a ripe old age, becoming stiff and partially blind before it died.

Bertie grieved for the lion for months after its death.

He decided to carve a lion into the chalk hillside so that the lion would live on and never be forgotten.

It took twenty years of hard work before the lion was finished.

Blue butterflies visit The White Prince carving after rain; they drink from the chalk face, transforming it into a living creature, the butterfly lion.

Questions

1.   Was Millie sorry not to have had children?

2.   What was life like for the lion at Strawbridge?
     Is this a good life for a lion, do you think?

3.   Millie did not let the lion sleep in her bedroom.
     Would you?

4.   How was Bertie affected by his leg injury?

5.   How did Millie, Bertie and the lion spend their Sundays
     together?
     Does this sound like a good life, in your view?

6.   Why did the lion never try to escape?

7.   What did the lion do when Bertie went out in the car?

8.   What poor health did the lion suffer from in old age?

9.   How did Bertie respond to the lion's death?
     Why did he respond this way, do you think?

10. What monument did Bertie choose for his lion?
     What made him choose this monument?

11. How long did the carving take?
     Was it hard work?

12. When do the butterlies come to The White Prince?

13. How do the butterflies transform this monument? Comment on this image.

14. What is the mood like as this chapter ends?

15. What illustrations would you choose to accompany this chapter, if you were the novel's illustrator?

Chapter Fourteen
'And the Lion shall Lie Down with the Lamb'

Summary

The boy asks about Bertie and learns that he has died and is buried beside The White Prince.

The old lady offers to drive the boy back to school before he is missed.

He asks if he can visit again and she says of course he can, adding that she may not be easy to find, but she will be there.

Nobody has missed him at school. Best of all, Basher Beaumont is in the sickroom with measles.

At supper, the narrator talks to his history teacher, Mr Cook, about Bertie. Bertie's name is under the East Window in the chapel. He was the only old boy ever to win the Victoria Cross.

Mr Cook recalls Bertie's widow unveiling the plaque. She died a few months later, of a broken heart. Strawbridge has been lying empty ever since.

The boy goes and reads the plaque dedicated to Bertie in the chapel.

He cannot sleep a wink that night, trying to puzzle it all out.

Questions

1.   What happened to Bertie?
How does this affect the mood of the story?

2.   Why does the old lady tell the boy not to look so
worried?

3.   Does the old lady in this story strike you as a typical old
lady?
Give reasons for your answer.

4.   Describe Millie's car.

5.   Why is Basher Beaumont in the sickroom?

6.   What does the boy have for supper?
Does this sound appetising to you?

7.   What does the boy learn about Bertie from Mr Cook?

8.   "The only old boy ever to win the VC"
What do Mr Cook's words here mean?
What is the significance of Bertie's achievement?

9.   What does the boy learn about Bertie's wife from Mr
Cook?
What does this mean about that afternoon's events?
What is your response to this?
How would you be feeling if you were the boy in the
story?

10.   What does the plaque say about Bertie?

11.   Why can't the narrator sleep that night?
        Could you, in his position?

12.   What would you do next, if you were the boy in this
        story?

Chapter Fifteen
'Adonis Blues'

Summary

The next afternoon the boy goes back to Strawbridge.

He knocks at the door, but gets no response. When he calls out, asking if someone is there, he hears a voice saying, "We all are", but when he turns around, he is alone.

He goes and sits on the hill and looks at the empty great house below him.

The rain stops and an Adonis Blue butterfly lands on his arm.

He hears a voice asking him to keep the lion white for them, so that he will not be forgotten.

The boy says he will and feels the earth tremble beneath him.

Questions

1. Where does Morpurgo (the narrator) go the next afternoon?

2. What happens when he knocks at the front door?

3. What happens when he calls out?
   How would you feel here, if you were him?

4. Where does he go next?

5. Describe the great house beneath him.

6. What is the atmosphere like at this point?

7. What happens when the rain stops?

8. What does the voice ask the narrator to do?

9. What happens when he agrees?

10. What is going on here?

11. Would you agree to the voice's request?
    Why/why not?

12. Do you like this ending?
    Give reasons for your answer.

13. How does the ending make you feel?

Further Questions

1. Describe Bertie's character, using examples from the text to support your ideas.

2. Describe Millie's character, using examples from the text to support your ideas.

3. Describe the narrator's character, using examples from the text to support your ideas.

4. What are parents like in this story?
    How do they treat their children?
    Do the parents in this story have a positive (good) or negative (bad) effect on their children?
    Give reasons for your answer.

5. Do you believe that something like the boy's encounter with the old lady could really happen?
    Give reasons for your answer.

6. Does the author depict the lion realistically in this story?
    Refer to the story to support your points.

7. Does the author depict war realistically in this story?
    Refer to the story to support your points.

8.   Bertie is dead against the idea of his lion being sent to a circus.
What makes him feel this way?
What are your views on circuses?
Explain your ideas fully.

9.   What does this story tell us about loyalty and friendship?

10.   Is this a war story, a love story, a ghost story, or some other kind of story?
Give reasons for your answer.

11.   What is the mood like as the story ends?
Can you explain what makes it this way?

12.   What lesson does the author share with us in the novel?
Is this a valuable lesson, do you think?

13.   Describe the time and place this story is set in (the world of the novel).
What is appealing about this time and place?
What is unappealing about it?
Include examples in your answer.

14.   What are the main themes/issues in this novel?
Explain your choices, using examples from the text.

15.   What did you like about this novel?
Include examples in your answer.

16.   What did you dislike about this novel?
Include examples in your answer.

17.   Who is your favourite character?
What do you like and admire about them?

18.   Which character do you dislike most?
Explain what makes you dislike them.

19.   What different elements of the story combine to make
this novel exciting?

20.   Do you like the ending?
Does the ending complete the story?

21.   Was there anything in the story that you would have liked
to know more about?
Explain your answer fully, including examples.

22.   Would this story make a good film?
What actors would you choose to play the key roles?
Explain your choices.

23.   What was your favourite part of this story?
Why did this section appeal to you?

24.   What is the most exciting part of this story?
Give reasons for your choice.

25.   What is the saddest part of the story?
Give reasons for your choice.

26.   How would you illustrate the cover of this novel?
        Explain your choice of images here.

27.   Does this novel remind you of any other novels, films or
        television programmes?
        Explain your choices.

28.   Would you recommend this novel to a friend?
        Why/why not?

Classroom Questions Guides

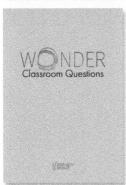